Safarnama

Anoorag Sunkari

BookLeaf Publishing

India | USA | UK

Presentation by *BookLeaf Publishing*

Web: www.bookleafpub.com

E-mail: info@bookleafpub.com

ISBN: 9789358310368

First edition 2023

ACKNOWLEDGEMENT

I want to thank all my friends and family who have supported me and encouraged me to write poems. I would also like to thank all my English language teachers who introduced me to the world of poetry.

PREFACE

In my journey so far there are different things that I have seen or experienced. I hope these poems will allow you to see life from a different perspective. I enjoy traveling, meeting people, and sharing stories with them. These poems are a collection of inspirations drawn from these experiences.

Stella

Open skies
Painted in blue
Surrounded by trees
changing their hue

Oblivious to all
Running carefree
With heart on my sleeve and
Tongue sticking out.

To the edge of the world
With my best friend
Up and up and up we go the rocks
To see the painted sky
Down and down and down we go the trails
To see the open waters

I follow you wherever you go
Falling asleep in your lap
You go out the door
I look for you out the window

O dear O dear friend
I'm where you are
You are where I'm

You are my best friend
Who is always by my side

Heartbreak

Last night,
under the blanket of stars they meet
With a throw, some coffee and loads of chatter

Reminiscing the old tales
They laugh some, then cry some
Their heart aching from within
 bleeding with the pain of heartbreak

Fighting the tears back
Holding onto each other's hands
They pour their heart out.
All about the seducer
Who showed the promise of love

Gazing into each other's eyes,
They smiled again as they did as kids
Promising not to fall
for the bastards with the broken promises

Winter

Snowy mornings,
Beanies and gloves,
Heated seats,
Warm coffee,
All set to go,
then I see
Dancing snowflakes stuck out my window.
With the sun shining, I smile and drive by.

Dream

5

I closed my eyes waiting for the gates to open
I could hear people talking
Kids crying, flight announcements
Everything fading away slowly
I open my eyes to find myself back home
Smell of homemade food.
It felt like I was lying in my bed back home
I could smell my mom cooking rasam
I opened my eyes only to realize I was still at the
gate
Waiting for my flight
I guess this is what going home feels like

To the Unknown

Hold my hand and walk into
the storms on a dark night
Across the dingy alleys,
Through the broken bridge
Far up the northern mountain
I take you to see a beautiful dream
Dream of open fields
Filled with dogs herding sheep
In our world of love faith and hope
Birds chirping,
squirrel running.
Oh my dear,
Standing in the shadows
I'll protect you
Saving you from your falls
Holding on to promises made to you
But oh my dear,
Don't you break your promises
I will hold you to it
I will never let go of you
That's for sure

Next Chapter

May arrived, exams reached their end,
The waiting game began, uncertainty increased.
Reality poised to strike, hope and dismay in its
wake,
Confusion and panic entwined, emotions at
stake.
Amidst the chaos, I woke to a verdict unfair.
Results before me, an arrow through my heart.
I had faltered, I had stumbled, failed to meet the
mark,
Failure embraced me with a heavy hand,
Expectations shattered, expectations unmanned.
Admission letter gripped tight in my palm,
Tickets booked, a new chapter, a healing balm.
With two bags, I packed my cherished past,
memories that I held dear,
Embarking on a journey, a new world awaits.

Simplicity

Soft sunlight caresses my cheek at dawn's
embrace,
Leaves transform, painting nature's vibrant
grace.
From sunset's allure to night's celestial hue,
A tranquil thread weaves these wonders through.
Basking in the golden rays of the sun,
Each scene whispers serenity, merging as one.
In life's humble joys, simple and pure,
I capture their essence.
Sunset whispers tales of beauty's descent,
Chasing simplicity, finding solace in every
fragment.

Unsaid Words

Beneath a sky where winds whispered with grace,
Fresh snow kissed the earth, a tranquil embrace,
She immersed in pages of a cherished book's prose,
While he nestled in her lap, finding sweet repose.
The crackling fire danced, a warmth they both share,
Its flickering flames weaving a cozy layer,
Occasional hums of their favorite Rafi song,
Filled the room, dispelling silence's throng.
Fingers entwined beneath the quilt's tender fold,
She gently asked, "Are we okay?", so bold,
He remained in her lap, gazing into her eyes,
Smiling, he assured, love's unspoken ties.
She closed the book, attuned to his heart's tune,
Its rapid beats echoed, a rhythmic commune,
In synchrony, their pulses danced as one,
A symphony of love, forever to be spun.
And there, in that cherished moment's embrace,
Their souls entwined, adorned with grace,
For within their bond, a love pure and true,
Their hearts beat together, a lifelong debut.

3 am Thoughts

In the depth of the night
the moon shines bright
it is all quiet and serene
my thoughts start to dance
the clock strikes 3 and sends me trance
whispers of dream
makes my heart scream
intertwined with hope and doubts, my mind
plots a scheme
Amidst this chaos, a spark ignites,
guiding me through the labyrinth of nights
Ideas sprout like stars in the night sky
In the calmness, creativity thrives

Oh, 3 am thoughts, both profound and deep,
with you, my soul embarks on a journey, steep
For in the twilight hours, I am truly awake,
Exploring the depths of my innermost lake.

Home

4 walls and a roof over my head
should we call it home, coz I am loved and fed
Is it the arms that embrace with love
or is it sleeping on the terrace with the night sky
above
Is it the laughs shared with the strangers
or is it the journey you took with them knowing
the looming dangers
Is it the lows and highs that you shared
Or is it the leap of faith you dared

It was a feeling, elusive yet profound,
A sense of belonging, where peace is found.
A sanctuary within, where the heart finds repose,
A refuge from the chaos, where true solace
flows.
In the depths of introspection, I discovered the
key,
That home resides within, waiting patiently for
me.
No longer seeking refuge in another's embrace,
I've learned to cultivate within my own sacred
space.

Amma

I see myself through her eyes
Running towards my dreams, without saying
goodbyes
She sees me for who I am
not giving the world a damn
Picking me when I fall
worrying when I don't call

Raised me to be good and strong
to stand and fight against wrong.
Taught me to be respectful and true,
honor everyone, regardless of their view.

To stand up for justice, to be a voice,
To make a difference, to make a choice.
taught me never to be scared
coz the people in the world are not squared

Her love knows no bounds,
Her influence in his life, it resounds.
She shaped him into the man he's become,
Her legacy lives on, her love never undone.

So here's to you, dear mother, my guiding star,
You're cherished and loved, just as you are.

Forever grateful for the love you impart,
In your embrace, I find home, a place in the
heart.

Walls

I don't have hidden wings that can make me fly
Far away from the sorrows that make me cry
I have got a room deep in my heart, where I go
down
the sounds and my thoughts don't reach the town
Walls scratched with my nails
the feelings etched with details
These turn into words, they make sense
these sound like poetry, they make sense
take a look at them, when you get a chance
get a peak into my life, which is spicer than the
salsa dance

Calm Down

In this celestial waltz, behold our bond,
As I, the moon, and you, the tide, respond.
Surging on the shore with all my might
A wild dance, a captivating sight

Yet, like a racehorse, you swiftly retreat,
Only to return with a fervor replete.
Painting the shoreline, creating our rhyme
In this eternal game, our cherished pastime

The sand is my canvas, like a child's playground
Bright under the moonlight, they create a sound
Dancing carefree till the sundown
The tide says Baby, calm down

For in this cosmic choreography we find,
An eternal connection, forever entwined.
So let us continue, bound by this delight,
Under the moon's gaze, shining so bright.

Life's tapestry

On twisty paths we embark,
From Malibu's embrace we start.
Through luxury our journey winds,
Over mountains, where beauty finds.
To Big Sur, where horizons blend,
Crossing oceans, our spirits ascend.
Bixby Bridge, a graceful stride,
Through redwood forests, secrets hide.
Waves crashing upon the shore,
Sun's glow on cliffs we adore.
Piercing clouds, painting the sky,
Life's masterpiece, we can't deny.
Such is the essence of our drive,
A scenic symphony, we arrive.

Will you be my anchor?

In the shadows of my mind, doubts find their
way,
Whispering questions, leading me astray.
Amidst the chaos, my confidence weaken
Shattered by the inner pains, I look for my
beacon

Like a tempest's gust, it shakes my foundation,
Clouding my vision, causing hesitation.
I question my worth, and my abilities, lying in
the kitchen
Wandering in the labyrinth of my thoughts, I
look for my beacon

I go looking in search of him
After my sorrows are filled to the brim
His voice stops my tears
His presence calms my fears

Oh dear, oh dear! What have I done
His love shines over me like the midnight sun
Drunk in pain, self-doubt begins to creep back in
Fighting my tears, I look for the answers within

Embracing the challenges, shine through the
night
I face those doubts with unwavering might
He gave me strength, showed me light
Whispered in my ears; darling, it will be alright

Is that me?

Blue eyes, hypnotize
hold on, that's the wrong start

Feelings all over like a bar chart
But looks calm before the storm hits his heart
Looks smart,
Gold heart.
This is the much-needed kickstart

Wears his heart over his sleeve
But don't think he is naive
Once you start talking, he won't leave
I don't think you still believe
I guess you gotta listen to the story from New
Year's Eve

Called all his friends, made a feast
They came from far, all the way from northeast
For his biryani and his anecdotes
Sharing a single malt, music on its last note
Reminiscing the good old days
He tells the stories, harping on their praise
Beaming with pride,
tears rolling down the cheek, with nowhere to
hide

The music fades out, and the silence makes him
fear
Saved by the clock striking 12, they all shout
Happy New Year

Lucid dreams

Shoot for the stars, they are in your reach
Sounds good in a Commencement speech
Up above the world so high
They shine like a diamond in the sky

Do you jump high and grab it?
Or do I need a permit?
Well within my reach
Can't park my ass on a beach

Is it easier said than done?
I gotta try harder until I've won
Did Krishna get it right?
When Arjun followed it with all his might

Do I chase happiness or dream?
This is my life's recurring theme.
Should I run a little scheme?
Make happiness my dream.

Heart and soul

My heart wants,
endless laughter
My heart wants,
Happy faces
My heart wants,
Endless conversations
My heart wants,
To be free.

But what does my soul get?
Happiness,
Memories,
Lifelong friends,
Gratification,
And some validation

Get ready to fight

Beaten and downtrodden
Fighting for his breath
Sucker punched
Swollen cheeks
Bloodied eyes
Ears ringing
But he heard one voice
Cheering his name
Rocky, Rocky, Rocky!!

He rolls over the mat
With all his might
Up on his feet
Guess standing up
For that one voice
Rooting for you
Was all that was needed
To continue the fight

Black and White

For pandas, playing with bamboos we saw some,
In her heart, a love blossoms.
Finding joy in their antics
Playing in the snow in a group of six

Found a giant one
That could be touched by none
Radiating smile like the morning sun
Every time someone mentions one
From clothes to shoes to earrings she would
always daydream
Her room decorated with the same theme

Her love so pure
She had so much strength there was only so
much she could endure
Seeing bei bei leave,
Her eyes couldn't believe.
But in her heart, he finds a forever home,
In her dreamland, he freely roams
Jumping in the snow and tumbling down the
slope
In her dreamland, he is still pretty dope

Angels landing

A frozen wonderland,
Where beauty expands
Silent and serene,
The landscape is so pristine

Footprints afresh on the snow
Whisper tales of those who chose to go
Frozen trails and snow-covered trees
Cheeks kissed by the cold breeze
With the temperature at below 0 degrees

The snow gleams bright under the sun
The mountains care for none
With each step to the top, a new world unfolds
With each step to the top, your resilience molds

The solitary hiker admiring the beauty from top
Better than his urban jungle view
Making memories along the way
Watching the snowflakes dancing like a ballet

Oh, Angels landing, I bow down to you
For your breathtaking trails and view

www.ingramcontent.com/pod-product-compliance
Lightning Source LLC
La Vergne TN
LVHW021343200726
843509LV00014B/2637